SPOTLIGHT ON A FAIR AND EQUAL SOCIETY

CONNECTING WITH OTHERS

MARY RATZER

PowerKiDS press

Published in 2023 by The Rosen Publishing Group, Inc.
2544 Clinton Street, Buffalo, NY 14224

First Edition

Editor: Greg Roza
Book Design: Michael Flynn

Photo Credits: Cover, pp. 28, 29 Monkey Business Images/Shutterstock.com; (series background) tavizta/Shutterstock.com; p. 4 ESB Professional/Shutterstock.com; p. 5 https://commons.wikimedia.org/wiki/File:President_Kennedy_inaugural_address_(color).jpg; p. 6 Halfpoint/Shutterstock.com; pp. 7, 26 Prostock-studio/Shutterstock.com; p. 8 Atstock Productions/Shutterstock.com; p. 9 grandbrothers/Shutterstock.com; p. 11 HASPhotos/Shutterstock.com; p. 12 https://commons.wikimedia.org/wiki/File:DeWitt_Clinton_Park_School_Garden.jpg; pp. 13, 18, 19 Rawpixel.com/Shutterstock.com; p. 14 Ron Adar/Shutterstock.com; p. 15 Jerome460/Shutterstock.com; p. 17 Krakenimages.com/Shutterstock.com; p. 21 antoniodiaz/Shutterstock.com; p. 25 Elena Elisseeva/Shutterstock.com; p. 27 Andrey_Popov/Shutterstock.com.

Cataloging-in-Publication Data

Names: Ratzer, Mary.
Title: Connecting with others / Mary Ratzer.
Description: New York : Powerkids Press, 2023. | Series: Spotlight on a fair and equal society | Includes glossary and index.
Identifiers: ISBN 9781538387955 (pbk.) | ISBN 9781538387986 (library bound) | ISBN 9781538387993 (ebook)
Subjects: LCSH: Communities--Juvenile literature. | Community life--Juvenile literature.
Classification: LCC HM756.R389 2023 | DDC 307--dc23

Manufactured in the United States of America

Some of the images in this book illustrate individuals who are models. The depictions do not imply actual situations or events.

CPSIA Compliance Information: Batch #CWPK23. For further information contact Rosen Publishing at 1-800-237-9932.

CONTENTS

CHAPTER ONE

COMMUNITIES

Communities come in many shapes and sizes. Your school is a community. So are teams, clubs, and religious groups. Groups of friends who all enjoy similar things, such as video games, **volunteering**, or swimming are communities. So are your neighborhood, your town, and your city.

When he was sworn into office, President John F. Kennedy famously said: "Ask not what your country can do for you—ask what you can do for your country." People in all communities must work together.

Some communities bring people together because of their interests. People who enjoy astronomy and watching the night sky may come together through this hobby. Fostering cats and dogs for a local animal shelter may bring people together. Music can bring people together. Celebrating **ethnicity** can bring people together.

Our planet is made up of communities of people, as well as animals, plants, insects, and other living things that interact and share a common place. What makes a community? What do all these examples have in common?

CHAPTER TWO

EMPATHY EVERYWHERE

You can explore your community and find evidence of **empathy** at work. Empathy connects community members. When people come together to work with and serve others, a community grows. When people share their talents, caring, and generosity with others, this action can shine a light on how healthy communities work.

Caring and empathy connect members of communities. During the COVID-19 **pandemic**, medical centers all over the world worked very hard to give tests, treat the sick, and give vaccines to millions.

Empathy can be invisible, and it may go unrecognized. It takes many forms. It can show itself as a huge force or an **isolated** incident. People's small acts of kindness may fill many needs. A student might shovel the sidewalk for a neighbor. A good cook might take a meal to a friend recovering from an illness. A gardener may share fresh tomatoes with a food pantry. Volunteer firefighters answer alarms. Community clinics help many people for low or no cost.

CHAPTER THREE

COMMUNITIES SOLVING PROBLEMS

There is a quote many people use when they're looking at problems or challenges within a community. "It takes a village" means that one or two people alone aren't always enough to guide and protect the children in a neighborhood. People may use the quote, "In numbers, there is strength," to describe how community members work together. When action is needed to protect something, for example, one voice is usually not enough. It also can take a community with a goal and a plan to welcome **refugees** fleeing from war and ensure that their needs are met.

A sign on a New York State senator's office wall simply states the call to connect with community problems: Speak. Stand. Show Up.

The members of a community may know more about problems because they see them firsthand. Many people need to communicate and call attention to problems concerning poverty, human rights, **equity**, or fairness. Change can depend on their words and actions.

CHAPTER FOUR

COMMUNITY SCHOOLS

Schools bring kids and families together. The shift to community schools expands the role of the school beyond education. Many kids have families with needs and challenges that affect every aspect of their lives. Schools may meet those needs and challenges in a familiar and trusted setting and connect problems with solutions.

Many schools already have programs that address hunger and basic needs for their students. The school serves as an **ally** for the community. Through volunteers and other local resources, a community school also supports the needs of students' families. Community schools connect families with support and resources beyond just school-based assistance. These services and programs help make sure that families have a path to make the connections they need.

Connecting community schools with local food pantries and service agencies meets the needs of many families.

CHAPTER FIVE

COMMUNITY GARDENS

Community gardens are a great example of how to connect with others. They start with a purpose. People in many neighborhoods have transformed their space, their health, and their alliances by developing gardens. Volunteers share in the effort and the benefits of using available, often neglected, spaces for gardens. In communities where fresh produce may be rare in stores, community gardens may come alive with fresh produce and healthy plants.

DeWitt Clinton Park in New York City opened in 1905. It included a community garden for children. Children learned about plants, **conservation**, and nutrition. The success of the DeWitt Clinton community garden inspired other communities to establish gardens in neighborhood parks.

Connecting **diverse** volunteers taps into diverse talents and launches a team effort. Not only are green beans, tomatoes, and other produce part of the payoff of a community garden, but so are new friendships and shared experiences. Many towns establish gardens for community members to use. People plant and harvest alongside others with a common purpose. Sometimes T-shirts, signs, and murals are used to call attention to the community effort.

CHAPTER SIX

THE GOLDEN RULE AND REFUGEES

A sense of community depends on treating others as you would wish to be treated. That has been called the golden rule. Many cities and towns in the United States have opened their doors to refugees seeking safety and freedom. Many people have fled Afghanistan, and the war in Ukraine is driving millions from that country.

During the war in Ukraine, many communities in the United States and around the world shared their goodwill through action and support.

Connecting with hundreds or thousands of **desperate** people who have lost everything challenges communities to treat others as they would wish to be treated if they faced a **crisis**. Communities can provide homes, food, jobs, language lessons, toys, and clothes. College campuses may open their student apartments and meal services to refugees. People may set up centers for free access to services. This model of generosity, empathy, and hope can provide a light in the darkest hour for those who need a place to begin again.

CHAPTER SEVEN

WELCOME!

Learning how to connect with others can build communities from strangers occupying the same space. The goal of safe, welcoming communities requires relationships and emotional connections. People in communities share common experiences and interactions. Reaching out to others is a welcome sign that invites a connection where there was none before.

Imagine that a family moves into a new house in a strange town. How can they begin to meet people and build positive relations? Perhaps the family puts out a dog dish filled with fresh water by their sidewalk. Soon people with thirsty pets begin to stop by routinely and the family begins to make new friends. It can be that simple.

Volunteering at school or in the community creates opportunities to connect with others. You might help collect cans for a school fundraising project or help other community members clean up a roadside.

Have you ever been new to a place? A positive attitude and relationship-building skills help create connections with others.

CHAPTER EIGHT

RELATIONSHIP-BUILDING SKILLS

Learning to connect with others is often best accomplished through experience and interaction with many different people. Reflection on how positive relationships take shape is a part of growing self-awareness. Learning from experiences that were positive and experiences that were **negative** builds social awareness.

You can build positive relationships with tools like respect, communication, support, and listening.

Friendships can help you learn more about relationship skills. Trust builds confidence and communication skills. Conflicts can be growth opportunities as friends resolve their differences in a positive way. Active listening contributes to understanding another person's **perspective** and can lead to empathy. Cooperation and **collaboration** are relationship skills that are lifelong assets. Supporting another person and sharing feelings are relationship building blocks.

Relationships require you to reject **stereotypes** and negative social pressure. Standing up for others and being an ally are strong relationship skills that are driven by values and character.

CHAPTER NINE

SOCIAL AWARENESS

Add social awareness to relationship skills and you have the power to connect with others. Since communities are based on connections with others, they depend on their members being socially aware and having relationship skills. Experience, curiosity, open-mindedness, and positive attitudes develop social awareness.

Social awareness is the ability to understand the perspectives of others and to empathize with others, including those from other cultures and backgrounds. Socially aware people recognize the strengths in others and choose to respect their feelings. They understand the cues that reveal feelings, including facial expressions, words, and posture. When you focus on other people, social awareness encourages connections and relationships.

It can be a sign that someone's becoming more socially aware if they begin to think more of others and become aware of their emotions and needs.

Connecting with others means that you understand their feelings and give them support.

CHAPTER TEN

ACTIVE LISTENING

Communicating with another person seems simple enough but can be challenging. Many people are thinking of what they want to say next when another person is speaking with them. When thoughts, feelings, and beliefs are involved, listening is more important than ever. Building relationships relies on respectful attention to the other person so you can understand them.

Active listening is a skill that you can practice and master. Start with paying attention. Focus on the other person. Show them that you're listening with eye contact and facial expressions. Respond to what the person said with feedback. You may wish to restate their point to be sure you understand. Hold back any judgment and ask open-ended questions to be clear about what you heard. Asking questions shows you are interested and want to respond with respect.

American psychologist Carl Rogers and his team developed ideas about active listening in the 1940s and 1950s. He and fellow researcher Richard Farson coined the term in 1957.

CHAPTER ELEVEN

CONFLICT RESOLUTION

Communities aren't conflict-free zones. Disagreements, opposing viewpoints, arguments, and anger may be part of daily life in some families, neighborhoods, and larger communities. Different points of view can lead to words and actions that drive people apart instead of pulling them together.

Recognizing conflict might take a little courage, but ignoring it only makes it worse. Understanding the issue or problem is key to resolving the conflict. Communities or even two friends who disagree may need to come together and discuss the problem and identify options to solve it. Once people reach a solution, making it happen takes both sides working together. Determining if the solution is working is part of the resolution. They might need another answer. Rebuilding relationships after conflict can be difficult, but it's worth the effort.

Schools can teach conflict-resolution ideas to students to help them build healthy relationships in school and in the community.

CHAPTER TWELVE

ONLINE COMMUNITIES

Technology has expanded the meaning of community to include the connections that people make online through social media groups, special interest networks, blogs, bulletin boards, forums, and instant messaging. Because of the COVID-19 pandemic, many businesses and groups turned to Zoom, Google Meet, and other services to carry on. Online communities grew out of necessity in a more **virtual** world.

Online platforms such as Zoom allowed some people to meet and go to school during the COVID-19 pandemic. They also allowed people to continue to make connections with others.

Schools sometimes offer online communities that support learning with collaboration, creativity, and communication. Many young people become part of online communities where they develop relationships and connections. Getting to know someone new works online as well as in person. Online communities grow as members share, play, create, and pursue strong interests. However, just like in person, online communities also can be unsafe or have negative aspects. Staying safe means staying smart.

CHAPTER THIRTEEN

BUILDING COMMUNITY IN SCHOOL

Feeling that you belong is a positive and important thing. Being a part of a good school community should encourage you to feel safe and allow you to concentrate on learning. Some teachers and other staff may greet their students at the door every morning. Teachers can encourage kids to get to know each other in a number of ways. Some schools have homerooms in which a student belongs to that group and has that same teacher for years. Trust and confidence can support kids on good and bad days.

Opportunities to belong to your school community may be waiting for you.

Kids may also find a community by engaging with a club, a music or art program, a sport, or a volunteer project. Collaboration, circle talks, connect time, and morning meet ups may all open the lines of communication and recognition that makes communities thrive.

CHAPTER FOURTEEN

GRATITUDE

Belonging to a community can be a positive force for everyone. Investing in the social and relationship skills that make your community thrive may inspire gratitude in others. Being grateful for the positive experiences and benefits of communities keeps you aware of the power of connections with others.

In one example, a mom in Massachusetts became very sick. Many people were an active and generous part of the community and stepped up to help her. They volunteered to make dinners, walk her dog, pick up her kids, do the family's laundry, clean the house, and drive her to treatment. Organizers had to create a schedule because there were so many helpers. This support lasted for years.

You can be a person for whom others are grateful. You can be a person who belongs and forms positive connections in the community.

GLOSSARY

ally (AA-lie) A person or country associated with another for a common purpose.

collaboration (kuh-laa-buh-RAY-shun) The act of working with others.

conservation (kahn-suhr-VAY-shun) Planned management of natural resources to prevent damage and pollution.

crisis (KRY-sihs) A difficult or dangerous situation that needs serious attention.

desperate (DEH-spuh-reht) Showing great worry and loss of hope.

diverse (duh-VERS) Having many different types, forms, or ideas.

empathy (EM-puh-thee) Ability to understand and share someone else's feelings.

equity (EH-kwuh-tee) Freedom from bias or favoritism.

ethnicity (eth-NIH-sih-tee) The quality of belonging to a group made up of people who share a common cultural background.

isolated (I-soh-lay-ted) Occurring alone or once.

negative (NEH-guh-tiv) Harmful, bad, or unwanted.

pandemic (pan-DEH-mihk) An outbreak of a disease that occurs over a wide geographic area and typically affects a significant proportion of the population

perspective (puhr-SPEHK-tihv) Point of view.

refugee (REH-fyoo-jee) Someone who flees a country for safety (as from war).

stereotype (STAYR-ee-oh-typ) A fixed idea that many people have about a thing or a group that is often untrue or only partly true.

virtual (VUHR-choo-wuhl) Occurring or existing primarily online.

volunteer (vahl-uhn-TEER) To do something to help because you want to do it. Also, someone who helps without expecting payment.

INDEX

PRIMARY SOURCE LIST

Page 5
John F. Kennedy delivers his inaugural address. Photograph. January 20, 1961. Washington, D.C. By U.S. Army Signal Corps. Now held at the John F. Kennedy Library and Museum, Boston, Massachusetts.

Page 12
Children's garden area. Photograph. 1906. DeWitt Clinton Park, New York City.

Page 23
Carl Rogers. Photograph. Natalie Rogers.